My Horse, The Hummingbird and A Very Small Tiger

A True Story for All Ages

by Amita McBride

Illustrations by Samuel Bacon (my son)

Photos by Amita & Galloping Grace Youth Ranch

ISBN 978-1-953699-49-7 (softcover)
ISBN 978-1-953699-50-3 (ebook)

Printed in the United States of America.

Book Vine Press
2516 Highland Dr.
Palatine, IL 60067

A true story as stories go, except for Tails the Tiger. You see, he is real too, but this is where imagination comes into play with the story. It will make more sense to you very, very soon...

My interaction with one of the smallest and most extraordinary of beings, the hummingbird, inspired this story. May you hear the soft voice of your heart and have the courage to follow the music within you. Trust there is guidance along the way, often where you would least expect to find it. My son, Sam, joined me in the telling of this tale by drawing the illustrations of the Hummingbirds for me. Thank you all for sharing your lives with mine through this story. May you feel joy for our natural world, an expansion within your heart, belief in yourself and your dreams. Give to life fully and without expectation, thus opening the doors to receiving blessings in return...and much, much more.

With tremendous gratitude, Amita

Grant Wade & Joe at Galloping Grace Youth Ranch

I would like to thank my horse, Joe. You are my heart, my best friend, my teacher and my dearest companion. The love and years shared with you have nourished me inside all of my deepest places. Thank you for gracing my life. This poem is dedicated to you.

What can reach into one's being like love?
She dances and moves us comforting and
warming like the rays of the sun
on a clear and gentle Spring morning.
Etherial and physical,
a perfect blending of the worlds
into ONE extraordinary breath
of deepest Knowing and Peace.

I met Amita while walking the Camino in Spain in October 2014

She showed great kindness and caring to me, a total stranger.

We forged a powerful bond and kept in touch while she steadfastly continued on the road to Santiago and beyond to the Sea. She made this arduous journey heading into the Winter walking in very difficult weather while working through physical pain and tremendous emotional hardship.

Amita constantly exudes courage and fortitude and has profound insight on life. She walks with with grace and acceptance which for many would appear an unfathomable hope for the future.

I have since learned that Amita has suffered many times during her life, in many ways and yet, as this book will attest, she has never lost her faith in the power of love and always following your heart, often when you don't know where that might lead. This book is an inspirational read bringing hope and light in both beautiful and difficult times. For those who are curious, adventurers, fearful or struggling, this book will bring great comfort, laughter and engender courage. Her love of animals and nature is profound. This story about her beloved horse Joe and their relationship is a testament to her spirit and her love and gives the reader a glimpse of her amazing connection with the animal world. She has a heart of gold always willing to help those in need regardless of what is transpiring in her own life.

Amita is amazingly talented - Very knowledgable in Amazonian healing plants, a glass blower, and a sacred mayan cacao creator among many other things - she creates beauty wherever she goes while living with great challenges her beautiful heart carries.

We remain close friends to this day despite being separated by an ocean.

I am proud to call her my friend.

Helen Thompson
October 2020

Amita Carder McBride

I was born Amanda Carder Welles. Many years ago, I partook in an extremely powerful earth ceremony. Through that experience and some remarkable events that followed, the Sanskrit name Amita was gifted to me.

I legally added Amita to my birth name, Now many years later, after feeling a deep pull to change my last name to McBride, the last name of my maternal great grandmother, I have done so.

I traveled to Scotland some years back in search of my roots. With the help of an older Scottish woman, the owner of a B&B where I stayed along my way, I found the answers. The McBride's originated from the Isle of Aaron. I also learned other information about the clan McBride.

My great grandfather had told me that I was a McBride and to not ever forget that. He added, where did I think my blue eyes came from?

Carder comes from my great great grandfather, Frederick Carder, the gifted artist and creator.

On this next leg of my life journey, I now step forward as Amita Carder McBride.

My Sonflower

Acknowledgements

This story is dedicated to life, the magic of all things big and small and the one heart that connects us all.

I would like to thank Helen Thompson for her friendship, unconditional love and for her tender heart. She is the dearest friend one could ever hope to have.

I would like to thank Emma Watton for the beautiful forward dedication and for the years we shared together. May her journey be great.

I would like to thank Max and Michelle Wade, the owners of Galloping Grace Youth Ranch, for their vision, their integrity and hard work in helping to make this world a more beautiful and healing place for the children, the horses and for us all.

This is my first published book. I would like to thank the readers for your support and your kindness with helping me to share my dream. I hope that in writing and sharing this story with all of you, I am in some small way helping to support you in the creation of your dreams.

Back cover photo: Phoebe Davis & Kaley Koester Loving Joe at Galloping Grace Youth Ranch 2011.

Knowing Amita - Foreword

For one to realize how significant the impact of this book will be, it is useful to understand the absolute truth it expresses. I am a young woman from the bustling streets of London, who sitting in the serenity of Amita's backyard, amongst the pine and oak trees, takes great honor in writing this foreword. In each of our lives we encounter milestones that give us the capacity to realign ourselves with who we are and where we are going. If we find the courage to act, we may open into richer, fuller versions of ourselves. For me, meeting Amita is one of these milestones.

I followed the inner voice of my heart to the United States. I wasn't absolutely certain as to why or how I would do this, but I trusted my knowing that it was for my highest good and took action. Upon meeting Amita, I realized that she was the reason I had travelled here. I feel immensely comforted by her openness and integrity. She is very easy to trust.

Before I met Amita, I had read a lot about spirituality and had begun to listen to my intuition. I had not fully opened into myself because the lack of solid experience shadowed my mind with many doubts concerning my ability to connect with the deeper aspects of awareness. However, after spending time with Amita, I have come to know the significance of the connection between how we think, feel, and act, how we see ourselves in relation to nature, to one another and to everything and how this is a direct reflection of our health and the lives we lead. Observing these things uncovers our belief systems; the potentially limiting filters through which we see the world. I have seen how Amita recognizes energies and can connect to different fields, working with people when they ask for her help in realigning their intentions, belief systems and patterning, in order to manifest positive changes in their lives. She helps with the shift into being more liberated and harmonious. How people interact and see the world changes because they align into their more authentic self. Basically, they stop being afraid to live and as a consequence, stop being so judgemental of themselves and others.

Amita sees differently from anyone I have previously met. She can observe and identify energy in people and situations and her connection to spirit and the Earth is crystal clear. She has shown me through experiential examples that life has an amazing way of supporting us and guiding us when we ask. She shared her cacao (chocolate) with me in various ways, including through ceremony, connecting me to the rainforest, experiencing the nutritional value of cacao and realizing that the Earth provides us with all that we need. I felt undoubtedly received by nature and the subtler, powerful realms of existence through different types of ceremonies and teachings. I am finding it easier to notice signs that I once thought were subtle but are actually incredibly obvious now that I am paying attention to them. I have witnessed how Amita listens, feels and receives messages and watched how accurately situations unfolded. It is paramount that she lives her life in awareness, listening to her inner voice and working on many levels all the time.

I was so excited when Amita shared this book with me because it is intended to help raise the consciousness of the readers by gently reconnecting them to the path of their hearts. She plays a crucial role in this world and this book is just one expression of that. I was interested to learn that Amita had originally set about writing another book, when her experience with the hummingbird guided her to write this book first. She listened to and acted upon that knowing. One of the things I have learned from Amita is that timing is everything. This is the perfect time for her to share this story with the world. Over this past year, essential factors have fallen into place to assist her in writing her original book now; one that has been developing over the past several years. The fact that she is inviting the readers to write about positive changes in their lives is a testament to her genuine caring about others and including us all in remembering our true nature.

We have shared at length about our lives. Amita's path has been filled with the kind of challenges one reads about in fiction novels.

She has demonstrated tremendous courage and pushed through obstacles that in some cases could have been fatal. Her determination, patience and tenacity have kept her on her remarkable path, resolute in her knowing that her experiences were training for her life's purpose and not, in fact, intended simply for suffering.

When I arrived as a stranger at Amita's door, she rescheduled her plans and welcomed me to stay for a month. She sees who I am and opens her heart to me, as I open my heart back to her. She helps me to see the gift in every moment and just how much there is to be grateful for. I will be leaving Amita's house as a much stronger person than when I arrived here just four weeks ago. She provided me with a safe space where I have been able to see and shift some of my patterns. I have dropped my hardness allowing my heart to open more. I have realized the misplaced feeling of anger I have been harboring deep inside of myself for years and have begun to shift it. I now see how this has manifested in ways that have prevented me from being who I am and who I want to be. I have greater clarity than ever before. She helps me to empower myself. Words cannot describe how genuine it is to be in Amita's presence.

I have great respect for the special way Amita walks her path, overcoming adversity while remaining positive. She gives her time and love so freely to those around her. Her ability to see, to heal and to teach others is an inspiration. Her message of truth and beauty is reflected in this story and expressed in the way that she lives her life. May we all realize how truly supported we are by life. When we open ourselves through the gifts of listening and have the courage to act, we allow the seeds of our fullest potential to blossom.

Emma Watton
London, England
August 2011

Contents

Joe and I at Galloping Grace Youth Ranch after giving him a bath 2011

Leaving Home

Have you ever tried to convince a mama goat and her baby to get on a horse trailer, or even a llama for that matter? Not an easy task I can assure you.

You see goats and llamas are very smart and they know how to be stubborn and refuse to do something that they do not want to do, especially if they are feeling nervous.

Starting at the beginning of this story would bring us to an afternoon on a beautiful late Summer's day.

I was trying very hard to talk my mama goat Daisy, her baby girl, Duchess and Moose the llama into getting onto a large horse trailer. Luckily, the people who they were going to live with were helping also. I even showed the animals how to step on and off of the trailer by walking onto and off of it myself over and over again. I must have looked rather ridiculous and I imagined them thinking, "Why does she want us to watch her climb into and out of that box and why would we climb into it when she is doing a very good job all by herself?!"

I started laughing out loud realizing how funny I must have looked. I stopped for a moment. I wanted all the animals to feel calm and safe and trust all the changes that were happening. I knew that they were all nervous because I was nervous and this was not helping matters at all. You see, Daisy was friends with my horse Joe or Grandfather as I call him. She and her baby looked to Joe to make all the decisions during the day and followed him everywhere he went. She was not too happy with being separated from him, leaving the home she knew, where she felt safe and knowing what to expect each day. She was not pleased, not one tiny bit. I talked with her and told her about her new home and all the new animals she would be with: horses, a pot bellied pig and many others. I assured her that she was going on an adventure! I told her she was strong and able to take care of herself, that she did not need Joe to make her choices for her. She looked at me as if to say, "Amita, I really am not interested in your offer. Could you please just bring us some oats?" I laughed out loud at myself yet again.

There was, in fact, MUCH change brewing for all of us <u>that very night</u>! A new life journey, as I was going to be loading Joe onto the very same trailer and taking him all the way to New Mexico from the mountains of Arizona for a very special assignment. His destination…a ranch, a very unusual ranch, a ranch known as Galloping Grace Youth Ranch. He was going to be working with children together with some other very special horses.

Galloping Grace Youth Ranch is owned by a wonderful family with four children of their own, who all work very hard together. They have a dream of bringing joy and love to children through being with horses. Teamwork is the only way the dream of the ranch can happen because they receive all of their help from volunteers. This is how they can give horseback rides to every child that comes to their ranch. They are amazing, just amazing.

So you don't feel worried, let me explain a little bit more about why I was sending my animal friends to new homes. My life was changing as much as Joe's life and I always want the best for everyone in my life. I knew that Daisy would not be happy on her own without Joe or other animals around her, so keeping her with me would not be the best decision for her and her baby girl. So, because Joe had an important new purpose in his life, everyone was preparing for change.

Galloping Grace Youth Ranch 2010

Tails

Now, I would like very much to tell you a little bit about Joe as he has had a rather extraordinary life thus far and is himself rather extraordinary.

Oh, I am so sorry, just a moment please. Ah, hum, well...Ok, I have Tails here. <u>A very</u> <u>small tiger</u>, only 3 inches tall in fact, and he very much wants to help me type this story it seems.

Tails has helped me from the very beginning when I first started writing and first wrote this story on paper and in pencil. Tails held onto my finger and whispered in my ear from time to time, inspiring me with ideas while I was writing. As he is so small, you will have to be very patient with him as it may take him some time to help me type. I feel very honored to have his creative help in bringing this story to all of you. Tails came all the way from Peru, which is in South America, and he sits on my finger. He has a great deal to say about things, moreover, he wants his picture in this story book, so I will do my best. I must say, I am a terrible drawer, which is why my son, Sam, drew all of the other pictures in this book for you. I am sure many of you could do a much better job in drawing Tails than me.

He is woven from the hair of a llama. He has green eyes with a little bit of yellow above them, a red nose, a red mouth and brown bushy whiskers. His body has black stripes and he has black stripes on his tail too. He does have a bit of a frown on his face even when he is happy so do not let that worry you one little bit. He is a lot of fun!

Tails loves adventure, singing in the shower, talking to very small bugs and he loves, adores goat milk and cherries!

Oh, and my cats, he really likes them as two of them are beautiful girl cats, Pillow and Celeste. As for our third cat, d'Artagnan, well he and Tails love to get into as much mischief together as they can get away with. Yes, d'Artagnan is named after the Musketeers. He must have indeed been one in his last lifetime because he is always involving himself in daring adventures!

Tails, Guido (gee-dough) the llama and Blue the lion ready for their next adventure with D'Artagnan

Tails does not like tuna fish or licorice or lima beans at all! He is gagging right now just thinking about them. He loves to lie in the sun and watch the clouds float by and he is bilingual too. This means he can speak Spanish and English. Pretty incredible huh? He did live in Peru after all. He loves to play and chase butterflies, wanting so much to catch a ride through the sky on their beautiful wings. He has not been able to convince them yet though and oh! oh! He can stand on the tip of his tail and spin in a circle while reciting rhymes. Isn't that amazing? He is really a very interesting fellow.

Ok, Tails is very happy now! Even though his mouth has a frown. It is not what it seems remember? He is ready to help me continue with the story. Where was I? Hmmm...Oh yes! I remember now. Joe, I was telling you about Joe.

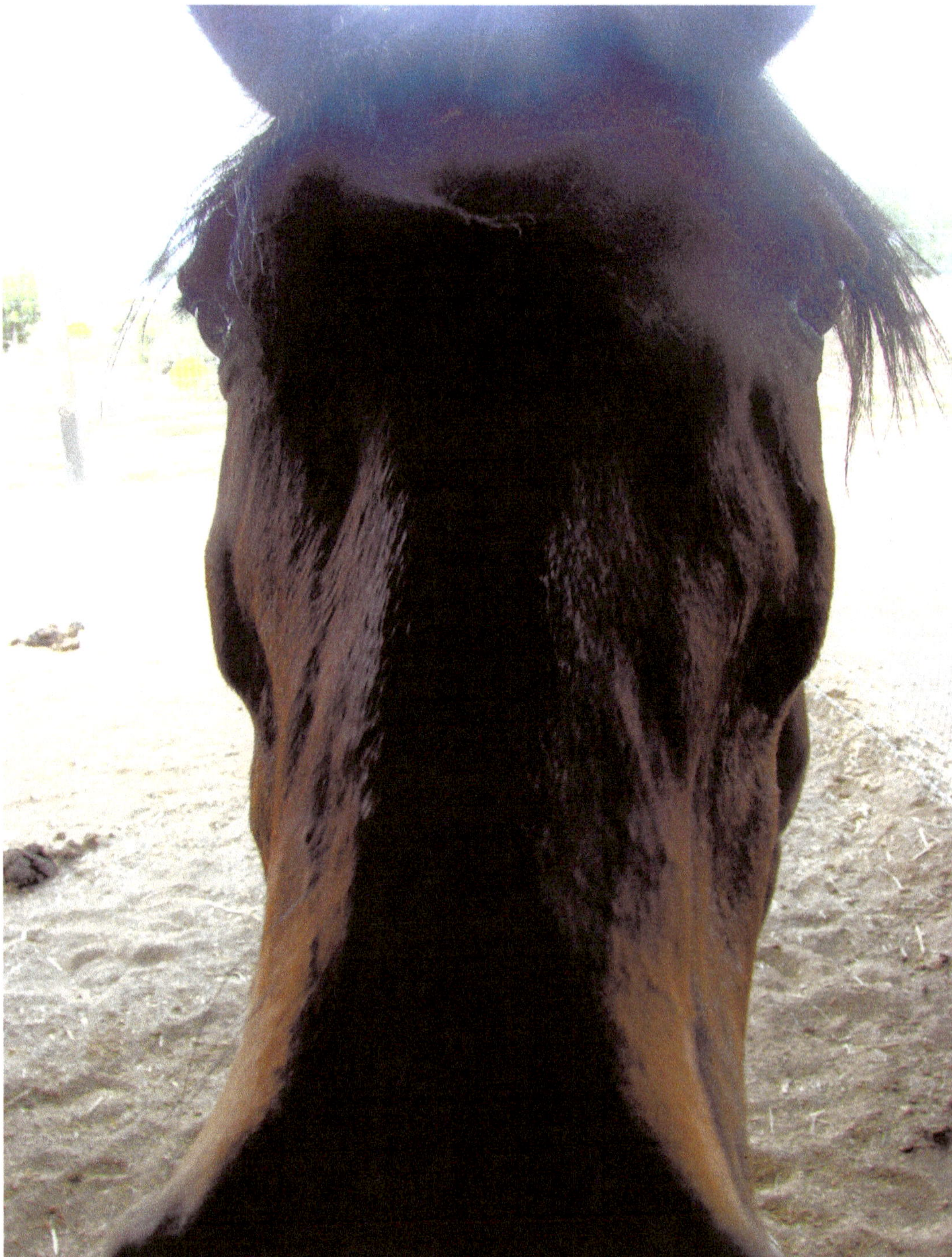

Joe

Joe is a mixture of three kinds of horses. You will have to use your imagination now as you read about all of the different horse combinations so that you can see him in your mind's eye. Ok, are you ready? Joe is part draft horse. You know the kind that are very big and have the huge hooves with all the hair on top of them and pull the enormous wagons? He is part paint horse which are the horses that have the big splashes of color on them like paint spilled on their hair AND he is part quarter horse, which are horses that are very fast and good at many things like competitions.

Joe is so handsome but he would never tell you this. He is too shy about such things. I bet you could not guess how old he is? First, you have to know a little bit about how long horses live.

Uh oh, Tails is jumping up and down on my finger to try to guess the answer! He is so excited he almost fell off my finger! Wow, I will now have to add that long distance jumping is also one of his many talents.

If you want to stop the story here and go read a little bit about horses, then you can come back and make a really good guess how old you think Joe might be. Tails and I will wait for you here. We will not continue the story without you, I promise.

Are you back? Ready to guess? OK, guess...The answer is incredible! Joe is 34 years old and in horse years that is amazing! It would be kind of like having a grandfather that is about 150 years old! Were you close in your guess?

I have fed Joe many special things over the years like green algae that grows in lakes and special plants that grow in the Amazon rainforest. These have helped to keep him strong and healthy. You can learn a lot about the rainforest if you want too as there are so many animals and plants that live there, more than anywhere else in the world!

Do you know what kind of animal this is?

A hint, I took this photo in The Colombian Amazon

Joe and I have been together for a very long time and he is my best friend. He has the biggest heart full of so much love and kindness that even people who are afraid of horses feel safe and calm being around him. The people at the ranch call him "Pooh Bear" because he loves to eat and take naps and because he is so gentle and kind.

When Joe first came into my life, he was not very well. He had been through some very difficult times and the veterinarian, which is a doctor for animals, was not sure if he would recover. He did not want me to keep my hopes up.

Just a moment please, if you do not mind, as Tails is getting upset. Let me just talk with him for a moment because it seems he is feeling worried about Joe and I want to help him keep his hopes up too! I will be right back...

..................Ok, I am back. You are very patient readers. Tails feels much better now. So back to my Joe. Well, I can be very stubborn and I knew in my heart that Joe would recover. I believed in him. I believed in my ability to help him and in the power of love and friendship. After some months of sharing time together, just sitting out in the meadow, taking long slow walks in the woods and eating healthy foods, Joe began to get stronger.

Amita in the Colombian Amazon. Oops, not my face and what a beautiful face indeed. (This animal and the animals on page 8 are called Three Toed Sloths)

A Little About Me

Tails would like me to tell you a little bit about myself. Hmmm, Ok but I should warn you ahead of time that I am rather unusual in how I see life and in how I choose to live my life.

All about me…well…let's have some fun with this question. I have boxed with a wild kangaroo in Australia who was trying to steal the apple I was eating and I won!

I have climbed Mount Olympus which is in Greece and is the home of the legendary Greek Gods. I climbed all of the Adirondack's 46 mountains in New York State by the time I was 15 and other mountains in different parts of the world. I have been hot air ballooning with the sun rising. I love riding horses and have ridden them on land, up mountainsides, in water and I even played a horse game called polo where you play on a team, riding horses very fast, using long mallets to try to hit a ball down a field and into a goal. I love traveling all over the world, meeting new people and experiencing life to its fullest. I love blue, orange and purple and all of the colors in between. I have called a falcon to my fist and taught people about birds of prey, like hawks, owls and falcons. I learned Spanish in a very small village in Central America, which is far, far away and I have traveled into the Amazon rainforests! I have swum in water in Australia where crocodiles live. I love cherries and beautiful warm people. I have raised goats and made yogurt and ice cream from their milk. I love bringing a smile to a stranger's face. I have walked through great challenges and I am still giving my best to life, even though on some days I am better at this than on other days. I even had a wild monkey climb up my body and wrap around my neck and I had to wait a long time for him to get off while he looked through my hair for bugs!

I did not have any bugs in case you were wondering. Tails is laughing hysterically right now. "Yes, yes just keep laughing Tails. You never know what may decide to happen in your life!" And, I have walked straight into a black bear who was picking and eating berries while I was hiking in Montana! We were both as surprised as each other and luckily for me, the bear continued on his way! So now you know a little bit about me and my adventures.

Joe and I out for a ride some years ago

More of Joe

Joe and I both began healing deep sadnesses through our friendship and love for each other. Our bond was like food for each other's hearts, the way water and sunlight are for the plants and flowers so that they grow strong and healthy. We started to play, a lot. We went on many, many rides together. We swam in mountain ponds, sat under trees sharing apples and carrots and we explored new places. Sometimes we rode with other riding friends. Joe's best horse friend was actually not a horse but a mule whose name was Macho. They used to play all the time. Once, after a long ride, my friend, Jessica and I, were sitting in the grass watching the horses. While Joe was napping, Macho snuck up behind him very quietly and with his lips, he carefully picked up some pieces of Joe's tail in his mouth and when he had a good grip, he pulled back hard! Joe jumped and Macho ran away making hilarious mule sounds all while Joe turned and chased after him! They ran all over the meadow together. We laughed so hard, we had tears in our eyes. Ok, Tails is gone, just gone. Oh my gosh. Where is he? Oh, oops, there he is all the way over there! On the floor! "Tails, Tails are you alright?" Hold on everyone, just a moment. I have to go and pick him up.................

....

Ok, He is on his back on my finger and he is just laughing and laughing. Hold on, let me just help adjust him...............hahaha, he is still laughing. Tails is completely adorable, I must say.

In the beginning, when Joe first came to live with me, he was very different from how he is now. It seemed to me that he had forgotten he was a horse, one of the most majestic, powerful and courageous creatures on earth.

Tails wants me to explain some of my words in case they are hard to understand. Majestic is a word that means something that is like a king, very royal and proud.

Courageous means being very brave and willing to face things that scare you. "Thank you Tails. I am so glad you are helping me write this story. Phew."

One morning, after Joe and I had been together for a few months, just as the sun was rising, I was looking out of my window while drinking my morning tea. To my astonishment, Joe began to run across the meadow as though he had just discovered that he had four long legs underneath his body! He was magnificent to watch, breathtaking as he let himself run! Holding his head and tail up high, he galloped slowly at first and then faster and faster and faster across the meadow, moving like the wind! I felt goosebumps all over my body as I watched Joe step into his strength. He was ready to live again, to believe in himself and let go of fear! Tears flowed down my face, spilling into my teacup. I was trembling all over my body with the immense love that I felt for Joe moving through me. That moment is forever recorded within my heart. I felt alive!

Tails is crying with happiness and roaring like tigers do when they feel strong and powerful. "ROOOAAAARR!" I know how he feels as in that moment while I watched Joe, I felt my own spirit soar high like an eagle in the sky, full of power and freedom to be who I truly am without fear, feeling as though anything were possible!

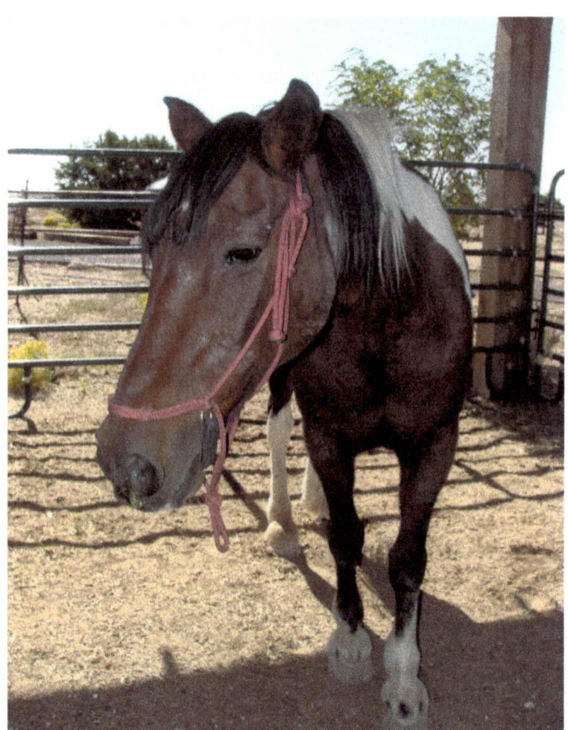

The Turning Point

Joe and I first met 12 years ago.

For the last three years of the twelve years in which we have known one another, I had recurring dreams where I saw Joe working with children. These dreams were very clear and detailed. I would awake from these dreams with goosebumps on my skin because they felt as though they were already true, already a part of Joe's life. However, every time I would go to talk with Joe about my dreams and ask him how he felt about this idea of working with children, he would put his ears back and turn around and walk away from me, sometimes trotting away. It was hard not to laugh because his response was always this way and when I did laugh, this would just annoy him more. It reminded me of someone putting their hands over their ears and shouting, "I can't hear you! Go away! I am not listening to you!" Tails is nodding his head in agreement. It seems that he has done this himself. He says that once when he was living in Peru, his other woven Tiger friends wanted to go swimming and he refused. "Tigers do not like water" he insisted and the more his friends tried to convince him to just try it, the more he refused to listen. Tails had never, ever even been in the water, so he had no idea if he would enjoy it or not. Well, it seems all his tiger friends came back and told him all about their adventures and amazing stories of their fun day, playing in the water, chasing dragonflies and lying in the tall grass in between exploring lily pads and other things along the water's edge. Tails had pretended not to be interested but deep inside he had wished he had gone with his friends and at least put his tail into the water.

So you see, Joe is special and he has a very special gift, just as each one of us is special and carries our own gift inside of us to share with the world. Joe can be stubborn just like we all can be stubborn when we do not want to do something or when we think we do not want to do something. Joe was very, very comfortable in his life just the way it was and he was not eager for any changes, especially not any big changes that would alter everything in his life as he knew it to be.

The unknown can be scary because we do not know what is going to happen. Sometimes, even if there is something in our lives that we are not happy with or it is not how we would like it to be, we can pretend we are happy because we are more afraid of change. We like to feel safe and know what to expect. Do you ever feel this way? Do you worry about things that are new or about trying things that you have never done before? Or do you just feel excited about everything that happens in your life?

Patagonia, Argentina - A Protected Reserve

Part of my life dream is for all of us to believe in ourselves, to help each other feel brave, to be grateful for life and all the experiences we have. This is how we learn about what we like and do not like, want and do not want, and how we learn about ourselves and our true passions.

I had made Joe a promise when we first met, that I would always watch over him and that I would always love him, that no one would ever hurt him again, ever. I do not make many promises, so this promise was a big one. This is still my promise to him. He deserves nothing less than all the love I have to share. There have been times, though, when I did not give him the time and attention he needed, when I got too busy or made other things more important. There were also times when Joe did things that were not kind or loving either. We grew together over the years, always forgiving mistakes and hurts. The trust between us is very strong. Joe helped me to love myself more too, not just give my love away to others.

The thought of not being with Joe sometimes brings me to tears. Yet, I also know he had so much more to give to the world and the world to him. I was going to help make this happen! I was willing to let him go because of my love for him.

Tails is asking me a lot about Love and what Love means to me... For me, true love is unconditional and this means you love someone for who they are and not who you would like them to be. This begins with yourself because if you do not feel love for yourself it is very hard to really love someone else from your heart.

Joe and I

Joe and I at Galloping Grace Youth Ranch 2011

Tails thinks this is very important too. How else can you know it is really love? You must feel it in your heart. You feel even more love when you share it! You feel so happy and you begin to see the world in a new way. Ok, I am just reminding Tails here that all of you probably know a lot about Love and I am sure all of you could share amazing experiences with us! So, now back to the story...

For the time being, I just let Joe be, knowing in my heart that whatever was supposed to happen, would show itself when the time was right. Time went by and we lived together as we had always done. Joe would come up to my bedroom door first thing in the mornings and call to me loudly, "mmmuuuuhuuuuuhhhhhh! Get up Amita!" I would pull my curtain back and with bleary eyes say, "Joe, it is only 5:15 in the morning!" He would not take "No" for an answer so I would get out of bed and open the kitchen door. He would stand with his head and shoulders in my kitchen and have breakfast with Sam and I. He would talk away and drop bits of grass, leaves, and fruit all over the floor. Sometimes he would stomp the kitchen floor with one hoof because he wanted to come inside. Try to imagine how that would look to have a horse standing in your kitchen having breakfast with you and helping himself to as many apples, pears and carrots as he could eat?

OH! Oh! Tails is laughing so hard he just fell off my finger again! Hold on just a moment here. I have to find him...uuummm. Oh, oh, phew, "There you are Tails! How did you get under my sock?" Hahaha. He is still laughing. Don't you just adore Tails?

Joe would also spend time with me during the day, standing with half of his body inside my office. My office is at home and the doors are wide French doors so he had a lot of room. He could have walked all the way inside if he had wanted. He would talk to me while I worked, napping too, from time to time. I loved his company. He does have an ornery side though. He has broken my bird bath, eaten all the bird seed from my bird feeder and broken a table by my front door with his hooves because he wanted me to open the front door and give him attention and I was not even home! He loved to pick up my sweeping broom and eat the bristles while shaking the entire broomstick all through the air. He cracks himself up. Can you imagine all of this? Joe can be pretty hilarious.

As time went by, as it always does, I was on a trip in Colombia, South America in the summer of 2010. Upon returning home, there was a phone message from a friend. She lives in New Mexico and told me about a horse ranch where she volunteered that worked with children and horses. She said in her message that she felt I may want to read about them.

My heart started beating fast and hard and I started to tremble. I knew this was it! I felt huge tears in my eyes as I knew this would be both the hardest and easiest decision of my life. I had to help Joe share his gift with the world! I raced to my computer feeling that if I did not act right away, I would not follow through with writing to the ranch. I would make a decision for the wrong reasons, selfish reasons!

The more I read about the ranch and the family, the more I liked them. When I read that all they ask of any child to ride one of the horses is to have an open heart, I felt so happy with the good that does exist in our world. They work for months each year to raise all the money to run the ranch, receiving volunteer help from people to make it all work. Horses eat a huge amount of food every day and they have 13 of them. Each child must help with some of the duties on the ranch as well as write a letter of gratitude as part of the trade for riding a horse at the ranch. The letters from the children are mailed to the people who have given to the ranch. Building confidence, responsibility and learning how to give are important aspects of the ranch's mission. I started to cry as I wrote to them, telling them about Joe and why I was writing, about my dreams and how truly very special he was, extraordinary to be exact. They responded to me right away and through my conversations with Max on the phone it was so clear to me that these were kind, humble, hard working, good people dedicated to their dream. It all happened so fast, too fast for me! After just a few phone calls and organizing the transportation for Joe, it was all set for only one week later! I was in shock! I had not planned on Joe being so far away when I had had the dreams in the beginning. I had always thought I would be able to see him often, that he would be close by. Now, often would not be possible with the distance between us. Maybe I would see him every few months at best.

I want you to know that I asked the ranch if they could have a llama or a goat there with the horses but they were only allowed horses. I knew in my heart that it was time for Daisy, her baby and Moose to have a new adventure too and that they would be in good homes with many other animals to keep them company.

Now, I had to talk to Joe. I knew this would be interesting from the last attempts I had made in trying to share my dreams with him. This was a reality now not just a dream and I knew in my heart it was right even though I felt my heart crumbling in places at the thought of him being far away.

He had Daisy and her baby as his own little animal family. Do you know that people used to stop and take pictures of Joe? They were amazed because Joe would lie down for his morning nap and let the baby goats leap on and off of his belly! They would do flips and acrobatics through the air as they jumped high off his belly like it was a trampoline! Joe would just lift his head and watch them. I have never in all my years of riding horses ever seen anything like that myself with any other horse, only with Joe. He would let Duchess sleep on top of his belly too, as he slept, all together with Daisy on the ground next to him. As I have been sharing with you, Joe is very special, unusual. I think you would like him very much. Whoops! Tails is gone! Completely gone!

He just flew off my finger while laughing so hard he got the hiccups! Hold on just a moment...I have to find him. Oh, hmmm, ok, there he is. "Tails, how did you land in the middle of my plant pot on the top shelf? You are covered in dirt now and still laughing I see." Back on my finger and just as happy as he could be. Tails, Tails, Tails...

Ok, where was I? Hmmm yes, yes. I went down to find Joe to tell him about the ranch. He saw the look on my face and he stood and looked me straight in the eye. He knew. It was understood. It was time. He trusted me. I also felt he was no longer fully satisfied just living his days with the goats. He seemed more irritable and bored and this was unlike Joe. It was time to expand his life. It was time for a journey, an adventure and I believe he was ready.

Look very closely on the ground near Joe.
Do you see anyone else there napping in the sun?

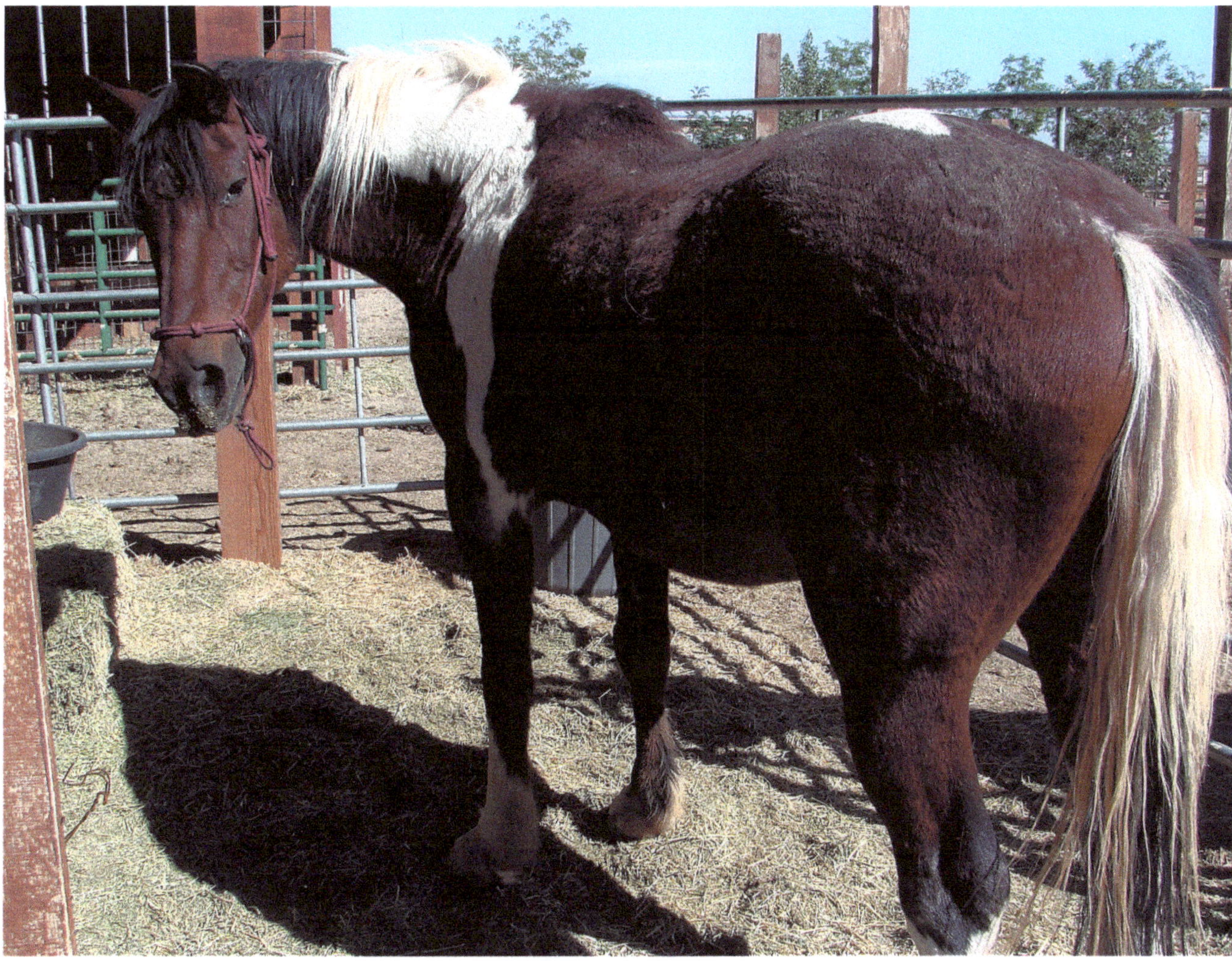

And where did you say my apples and carrots were exactly?

The Hummingbird

So, this brings me back to where this story first began, to an afternoon on a beautiful late Summer's day.

Remember, I was trying to talk to Daisy and her baby and Moose, the llama, into walking onto the trailer to go to their new home? Joe had not been on a trailer in many years and I did not know if he had ever been on one this big and with sides open to the outside. Daylight was going quickly and with the night following right behind, we had to work fast. Loading a horse onto a trailer is one thing, trying to do it at night is a very different kind of adventure that I did not want to have right then.

With Daisy nervous and unsure about the trailer, I ran to my tiny feed house to get some sweet oats for her. The door was already open as I had been going in and out for supplies. This time as I ran inside, breathing hard and rushing, up in the corner by a window that was not made to open was the most beautiful hummingbird! I stopped in my tracks. This had never happened before and the hummingbird was frantically trying to get through the window and back outside.

I paused, thinking quickly as my ladder was all the way up by the house and I did not feel I had time to waste because the hummingbird was growing increasingly alarmed and beginning to hurt herself by flying against the window so hard! She was so determined and focused on trying to escape through the false window. All the time, there was a big open door right behind her. She did not see it because she was focused on the light she could see through the window. She was quickly draining herself, so with haste...Oh, Tails is getting nervous with this part. I just need to calm him down, just a moment.......................ok, I am back. I hope you are ok too and still there with me. Are you nervous?

All right, so with haste, I tried balancing myself, not doing a very good job of it, on some feed bags with my right leg and with my left leg I stood on the edge of a large blue trash can that had all of Joe's winter supplies in it. I held onto the side of the wall with my right hand and reaching, reaching, stretching up, up, trying hard to reach just a little bit further with my left hand to help the hummingbird. She tried to escape my hand, fighting even harder against the window. I spoke to her with a quiet voice, telling her I was there to help her but she was too upset at being trapped. She did not seem to care about anything I had to offer as I was probably as scary to her as being trapped.

Her tiny mouth was now open and she was breathing very rapidly. I was not able to balance myself well enough to use both of my hands properly so I tried several more times with just my left hand to reach her. I was getting very worried about her and her struggle. I wedged myself against the wall and inched myself up just a little bit higher so I could use both of my hands to reach her. All of a sudden, she just stopped and collapsed on the sill of the window with her little head bent down and her wings opened out to her sides. She was breathing so hard, completely exhausted! She could not fight the window anymore. She could not fight herself anymore. She could not fight me anymore.

My hands gently cupped her tiny body and I carefully lifted her down to me as I climbed off of the blue trash can and feed bags. I then held her for a moment with both of my hands to make sure she was not hurt before letting her go. Tears filled my eyes with love and compassion for this beautiful little warrior. I turned and stood in the open doorway and then I opened my hands. She flew out of my hands, up and out into the sky, humming as she went, free once more!

My hands must have seemed terrifying coming towards her like that, like a strange creature, not knowing I was there to help her. As I stood there in the doorway for a moment, watching her go, I felt that I had just been given a blessing, a gift and an important message. A message not just for me, rather a message to share for all of us, including the hummingbird. A message that I was to write about and share with all of you.

I will tell you more about the blessing, the gift and the message in just a little while because as you know Daisy and Duchess and Moose and the people helping me were all still outside waiting! Oh, Tails wants everyone to know that he will offer to sit up on the window pane the next time I am working outside with the feed shed door open so he can keep his eyes open for hummingbirds taking a wrong turn. He will be a lifeguard for flying creatures instead of swimming ones. Tails is so wonderfully thoughtful, don't you think so?

I scooped up the sweet oats and ran back outside to everyone. I was feeling very different after my experience with the hummingbird, much calmer and more focused. Daisy went onto the trailer easily after that. We had to work harder with the baby who had never ever seen a trailer or so many people for that matter and she was not happy about any of it. We had to pick her up and carry her onto the trailer to be with her mom.

Then with Daisy and Duchess on board, Moose decided it would be safe to join them and he let me walk him up onto the trailer. I said goodbye and Joe just stood and watched as everyone was driven away to their new home, which was not very far away. It was down the very same road that I lived on and only a few miles distance.

Joe was oddly calm. He did not look for the goats, he did not pace, he did not call out for them. It was further proof for me that he was ready for change, perhaps not leaving our home kind of change but he was ready for some kind of change and only time would show us how much. I let him out to enjoy the grass and flowers. We spent the next hour together with me brushing him as he grazed, slowly combing his mane and tail, just spending quiet time together as the sun began to go down.

We were waiting for the trailer to come back.

I felt sad and excited all at the same time, one moment ready for the adventure and the next moment doubting myself. When the trailer came back, at first and just for a moment, Joe refused to step onto it. He was scared and pulled back away from the trailer very hard against the lead rope that I was holding him with. Then, he stopped and looked at me. He trusted me and I trusted him. He knew it was time to go. He then rather suddenly just walked onto the trailer as I gently urged him forward. I just kissed him and kissed him, covering his nose and face with love. I was rather startled and amazed as he had never loaded onto a trailer so easily before.

I fed him dinner because he was going to have to wait until 4am for us to leave. I did not want to load him after dark and I did not want to trailer him all the way to New Mexico in the dark either, so with food and water and plenty of room to move around, Joe was content and calm. I checked on him continuously as I was unable to sleep very much at all. I lay in my bed thinking about all the wonderful experiences and love I felt for Joe and how very grateful I was that he was part of my life. I also felt how quickly our time together had gone and this made me appreciate the blessings in my life even more than I already did.

A Moment of Choice

One late summer's day many years ago, I was driving up my driveway from an afternoon in town and casually glanced over my left shoulder, as I always did, to see if I could see Joe. To my utter surprise, he was down on the ground lying on his side, clearly in great pain. I was stunned. Turning the engine of the truck off, I walked over to Joe, desperately wanting to run, but knowing this would only stress him further if I did. My breath was short and fast and my heart was pounding so hard against my chest I thought it would burst through. Approaching Joe I could see immediately that he was in colic, meaning part of his intestines were twisted. Groaning, he was rolling, almost rocking his great body from side to side as he tried to soothe himself. There was an area the size of a grapefruit that was bulging on his left side. I walked over to Joe and knelt down on the ground beside him. I spoke to him in a soothing voice as I carefully placed my hands on the painfully twisted area to see if I could feel how bad it was. It was bad. I got up and went to call the Veterinarian. He came out right away and gave Joe something to help him sleep so that he could give him a gallon of mineral oil to drink. The Veterinarian wanted to make his intestines very slippery so that they could untwist. At least we had Joe on his feet and the hardest part was the waiting. The Veterinarian listened to Joe's belly and said that Joe had sand that had accumulated in part of his intestine from all the years of grazing in this area. He had seen it before in other older horses. Even though I gave Joe psyllium, which is a fiber that helps move food through, sand is heavy and had gathered in a section of his intestine and pushed it down.

The next day Joe was on his feet but he was not himself. He was not eating and for Joe not to eat, that just doesn't happen. He was clearly not feeling well, had not moved the sand through his intestines yet and the bulge was still visible on his side. I was worried. I worked on the knot for a long time, gently moving it and massaging it. I had played polo in highschool and we had two polo ponies that had had colic. It is a serious condition and not something you forget. I was in a state of utter concern for Joe and yet I believed in him, in his strength.

On the third day, he was back down. He was worse than before. I knew beyond any doubt that he was in real trouble. He was not fighting anymore, just laying on the ground, on his side breathing shallow, rapid breaths. I knew he was giving up. With tears flowing down my cheeks, I walked over to him and sat down by his beautiful face. I lifted his head, gently resting it on my lap. I lovingly touched him, talking to him almost in a whisper. My heart felt like she was breaking into millions of tiny pieces only held together by golden threads of love for Joe and wanting what was best for him even if that meant that I lost him.

As I sat stroking his nose, the sadness in my heart grew. His breath was more difficult and his eyes were glazed over. I felt a HUGE rush of energy move through me and I got angry!

I GAVE JOE AN ULTIMATUM, A DECISION TO MAKE.

"Joe, I said, "If you truly feel this is your time to go, to leave this world, I support your decision with all of my heart even though I feel like I am breaking inside. You are my family, my friend and we have walked through so much together. I would miss you and yet I would understand. If, though, you are choosing to give up, to stop trying, to not believe you can get through this, then I do NOT support your decision! I have not given into the hardships I have walked through and I am still here working hard. You would have me keep giving my life, giving my best while you give up!

I DO NOT ACCEPT THAT FROM YOU!

You must make a decision one way or the other as the pain of me not knowing what you are going to decide is too much for me. So please decide, please tell me Joe."

As I sat crying with my face bent over Joe, cradling his head in my lap, he looked at me for a long, long moment. Then in Joe's special way, he sighed. It was a very clear and determined sigh, "aghhhhhaaaahhhhaaaaagghhhh" and then he groaned and with tremendous effort he lifted his head and then his great body and he stood up! My mouth fell open wide and I leaped to my feet, throwing my arms around his neck while telling him that I knew he could do it and that he had so much more to give and to receive in this world.

I worked and worked on the knot in his belly and talked to him, reminding him of our adventures together, what it was like when he first came into my life and how much we had shared together. The knot released, it let go completely. He was through it. We had done it together!

Since that day, Joe has been different. I am not sure if I can explain it to you in words. He is stronger, more sure of himself. That experience was a gift. It was not easy to walk through but a powerful, life changing gift all the same for both of us.

Joe now eats a lot more psyllium to make sure that no sand can hang out in his intestines and get stuck again. The sand stays on the ground where it belongs and Joe is still with us right where he belongs.

Joe and I riding in Arizona

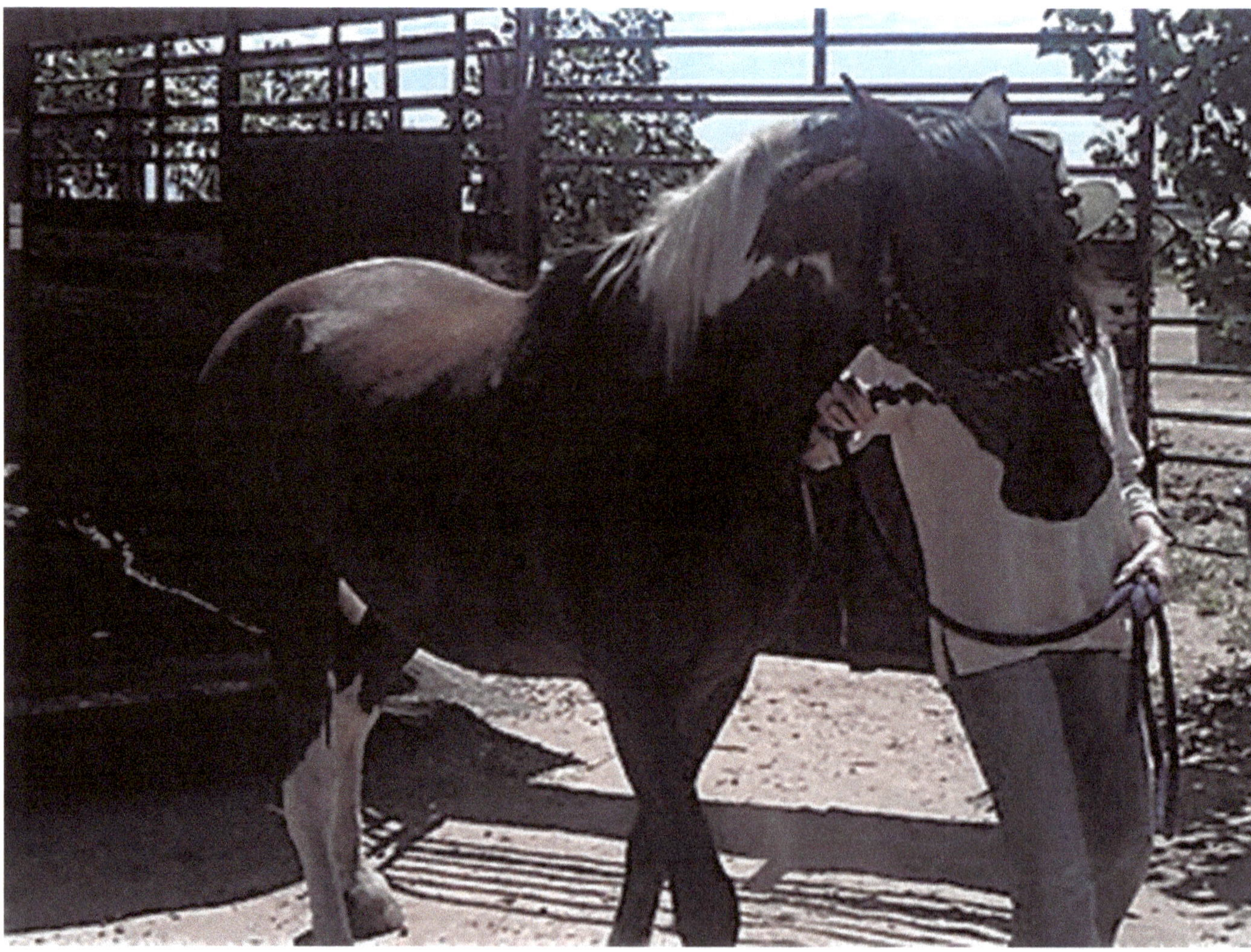

Joe and I arriving at Galloping Grace Youth Ranch 2010

Saying Goodbye

Joe stepped off of the trailer with his head up high. It had been a long journey and he had been nervous on the trip. He did not eat his breakfast and I had never seen Joe not eat his breakfast, not in 12 years!

Tails is giggling quietly. He knows how much Joe loves to eat and how much he does eat! Eating and napping may, in fact, be Joe's first and second favorite activities in life.

At the ranch, there were people everywhere and other horses in fenced corrals. Joe remained extremely calm. Max, the owner, was perplexed as he said that usually the other horses would all be at the fences eager to see the new horse, calling out and whinnying. All the horses were just doing their own thing as though nothing new or different was happening, like Joe was already part of the ranch perhaps?

Tails is crying. Now I am trying not to cry too. Hold on just a moment please.........He is telling me that he is so proud of Joe and I, Daisy, Dutchess and Moose for being so brave and strong. Tails has a very, very gentle heart and is easily moved to tears. I am a lot like Tails I think...What moves your heart?

After unloading Joe, meeting everyone, spending time being introduced to the other horses and having some time with Joe, I left and drove for another hour and a half to spend the night at my favorite mineral springs. I was already tired and it was quite a long drive but I knew being by the river and soaking in the warm mineral springs would be very good for me. I was going to drive back in the morning and have some more time with Joe before saying goodbye and making my way back to the mountains of Arizona.

When I reached the springs, I set up my tent and walked along the water. I sat under the stars and watched the moon for a long time. Being in nature always fills my spirit with peace. In the morning, as I began writing in my journal, as I try to do every morning, the hummingbird was in my mind and my heart. So was Joe.

Why was the hummingbird in my feed house at that exact moment? Do you have any ideas? How do you feel when you think about the hummingbird?

Sometimes, when we have changes in our lives like moving to a new town or changes with our family or even going to a new school, we can feel afraid and alone and even more afraid to talk about how we feel.

Sometimes, what something looks like is really very different from what it really is after all. Tails is very excited for me to share about his life changes because he was very nervous and scared to come to America all the way from a very small village in Peru and live here with me.

He wants me to tell you that he loves his adventure so much and none of the other woven tigers that sit on people's fingers that he knows of, got to have this kind of opportunity. An opportunity is when something new comes to our life and we can be open to it and do our best and have a new experience or we can be stubborn and stay still and not try new things because we are afraid of what might or might not happen.

What do you think the hummingbird was feeling when she could not get through the window? You see, the window seemed to be the way out because she could see the light of the sun, but it was something that was different from what it looked like, right? The window did not open and was not the way out BUT she continued to try harder and harder. That did not help her through the window either did it? Right behind her was a huge open door, much, much bigger than the window and this was the true path to her freedom.

She was too scared to stop and look around her to see what to do. So, then what happened? I came into the feed house and next to the hummingbird, I am a giant. Then, I reached up and wrapped my hands around her little body. How scary that must have seemed! But, I also was something that was different from what it seemed to be, right? I was there to help to free her but she did not know that. Only when she stopped fighting, could she receive the help she needed.

The feed house and I were both very new things in her life and she was terrified by the new changes. I thought about the times in my own life, when being in an unexpected situation sometimes caused fear to take over. It was not until I calmed down or exhausted myself trying to figure something out, that I was able to see the choices being offered to me. Sometimes even choices I was pushing away because they looked different from what I thought they should look like. Sometimes, I even chose the wrong thing, knowing I was doing the wrong thing! Hmmm, have you ever felt this way before? Tails sure has. He is nodding his head in agreement with great enthusiasm. He almost lost his balance on my finger again.

I believe everyone has felt this way as it is part of how we learn from life and mostly about ourselves. We can learn from other people, animals and nature. We can try to imagine how other beings see the world they live in. Imagine what it would feel like to be a hummingbird or a horse or a flower or yes, even Tails? Imagining what it would be like to be a very small tiger woven from the hair of a Llama is very interesting, don't you think? Using our imagination is really, really fun and VERY important. Imagination is how we create, how we play, how we share, how we dream about all the possible things we want to do with our lives. Don't you think so?

Joe chose to walk through his fear with a little help from me. I let him go so he could fly free and become more than maybe he thought was possible. Joe gave me the same gift in return. I have his pictures on my computer screen so I see him every day and this always makes me smile and fills me with courage to keep believing in myself and my dreams.

Renee Petrie and Joe. Galloping Grace Youth Ranch 2011

Joe is changing lives at Galloping Grace Youth Ranch just by being himself, "Pooh Bear with the Buddha heart," as they call him at the ranch. I have a very good feeling that he is also changing and growing in his own heart from the children who are trusting and loving him too. Together they are walking through their fears and opening their hearts more to new experiences and having fun, even if it is a little scary sometimes. Some of the people from the ranch told me that Joe is one of the favorite horses there of all the children and the volunteers. They wrote a story about him and put it on their website and they send me pictures of Joe with the children. I put some of the pictures at the end of this story for you. I want you to feel like you know Joe personally. I know he would love to meet all of you.

Kaley Koester Hugging Joe at Galloping Grace Youth Ranch 2011

As I complete this story, I am preparing to go and see Joe. I am so excited, I feel like Tails bouncing up and down on my finger! I have not seen him in just over five months and I am going to tell him about this story I have written in his honor. Joe is one of the most beautiful gifts that has EVER blessed my life. I miss him so much! I am going to take him all of his favorite treats, brush him, go for walks and just lay with him and watch the clouds go by. I can't think of a better way to spend a few days with my best friend. Tails wants to ride a horse now! He is so small but who I am to say he could not find a way. Oh, Tails says, "I could wrap myself up in the mane and hold on with my tail and say giddy-up. Or, I know, I know! I could sit in one of the children's pockets and then I could look out and see everything as we run, well, or maybe walk across the meadows. I know I could do it! I would like my own pair of cowboy boots too so I am a real cowboy!" "Tails, I have no doubt that you could do it and I would be there to cheer you on and support you!" The only thing I do not quite know how to explain to Tails is that he does not have any legs or feet so cowboy boots would be rather difficult unless we made one boot to fit over his body with a little hole cut out for his tail.

Tails's first ride with Joe! Galloping Grace Youth Ranch 2011

It makes no difference who you are, where you live, what you believe in or the color of your skin. You must follow your heart to find happiness inside of you. Then you can share it with others and love other people's dreams too. Dream BIG and just know you will fall down and feel scared sometimes BUT there is always a helping hand somewhere and sometimes not where you would think to look. It may not even look like a hand. "It could even be a tail," says Tails.

As we learn to believe in ourselves, and remember how to listen to our hearts, we will find strength because we will trust ourselves and love ourselves more and be willing to keep trying! Be open to life and all of her magic and mystery because you never know where she may lead you. Life is like a big river with many things to see and she helps carry us along, even waiting for us while we stop along the shoreline to discover and explore new things. Please remember one thing. When you find someone who is very special, appreciate and love them with all you have inside of you because there is nothing more powerful than love and nothing that can fill your life with as much joy than I have found. For me, being in nature is one of the special gifts.

I had no idea that my experience with the tiny hummingbird would become a story that I would write and share with all of you. I am so very glad that I did!

Thank you Tails for keeping me company, helping me with this story and being who you are because you are very special too. Especially, since I must use my imagination to have the most wonderful and playful conversations with you. It made writing this story all the more fun!

May we walk more softly upon our planet with greater love and kindness through our beliefs, our thoughts and our actions thriving with Thankfulness and Gratitude for all things, in all ways.

Claire Wade with Joe at Galloping Grace Youth Ranch 2011

Kat Rhodes with Joe for a fundraiser for
Galloping Grace Youth Ranch 2011

Ava Bilan riding Joe at Galloping Grace Youth Ranch 2011

From Left to Right: Phoebe Davis, Claire Wade, Kaley Koester with Joe at Galloping Grace Youth Ranch 2011

Final Reflections

Have you ever sat very, very still and watched a hummingbird?

Hummingbirds need the sun, nature, lots of flowers, open spaces and they need freedom to live just like you...

Did you notice in the picture my son drew of the Hummingbird flying outside under the sun that there was one flower that was different from all the other ones? Do you know what kind of flower that is? What do you notice about that flower? What does it tell you about life?

Have you ever ridden a horse?

Have you ever wondered what it would be like to be a horse?

Have you ever tried to imagine what it would be like to talk to the animals in their language? To see the world the way that they see it? How they see us?

Have you ever thought about how it would be to be very, very small in our world? How differently everything would look to you. Hummingbirds are very small. Tails is very small. Ladybugs are very small. Or how it would be to be very big? Horses are big. Elephants and Whales are big.

Have you ever wondered about why you feel the things you feel and where all your feelings come from?

Patagonia Chile 2007

Have you ever just lay in the grass, watching the clouds go by and just wondered about anything and everything at all?

Guido, The llama

I am dedicating this last page of the story to Guido (gee-dough) the llama who is also from Peru. He is extremely upset with being excluded from the story. I am so hoping that this last page dedication eases his distress. He wants me to help you to pronounce his name correctly. He is sounding it out for you now. gee-dough

(Please read the following in your best Irish accent)

"Well I would just like to say that all the glory is on that tiger, just because he's got stripes. Amita didn't even ask me to help her with the story and I've been sitting here watching her write it with Tails. I am packing up my Yerba Mate and my gourd and I'm going to stow away in Emma's suitcase when she returns to England (she wrote the foreword, Knowing Amita, and if you haven't read it, now would be a good time!) Then I'll hop on a ferry to Ireland as soon as I can. I want to meet the leprechauns and see if I can kiss the Blarney Stone for luck! I've been listening to cassette tapes to get the accent right. Wish me all the luck of the Irish as I finally head off to follow my dreams."

An Invitation To Share

I would like to invite, not only the children, but also the adults, ANYONE who feels to share their extraordinary story, to please write to me. Please share your stories of love and caring, whether for an animal, plant, human or other being and how this relationship is helping you open, grow and appreciate all of life more fully, (this does include bugs and all critters, as together we make this beautiful planet). Please express the most unusual and amazing ways in which your dreams are unfolding as a direct result of reading this book. I would be deeply honored to share our lives together in this way.

The joy in helping one another find the courage to listen to the wisdom of our hearts, helps us all become stronger, kinder and more united. As we are willing to listen and learn from nature's gifts and the magic of life, our hearts open more fully into the beauty of our place on Earth and what we are truly capable of becoming.

Please email your stories to: amita@rideswithfire.com

Tails spending time with the flowers, hoping to catch a ride on a passing butterfly.

Dare To Dream

Dreams like Butterflies
Courting and Dancing on the
Wind
Eager to Become
To carry their Essence
high across the Sky
Syreading like clouds of
chocolate and Spice
Into the Soul of the World.

By Amita McBride

Michelle& Max, Brooke, Claire, Grant & Garrett Wade.

Joe--a lovable, huggable teddy bear wrapped up in a horse's body. Since coming to live at Galloping Grace Youth Ranch, Joe has brought joy, giggles, and confidence to hundreds of young riders with his calm demeanor and amazingly gentle spirit. We feel blessed to know this incredible animal and cannot thank Amita enough for trusting us with one of her very best friends.

Max and Michelle Wade Cofounders, Galloping Grace Youth Ranch

Photo by Michael Tucci

Amita McBride is a gifted seer and pioneer who works with people, animals and the Earth helping to facilitate deep transformation and healing in all aspects of life. She has a passion to create the extraordinary, personally doing so through her own ongoing awakening. Amita successfully created Rideswithfire.com and her Sacred Raw Cacao (chocolate) line. Her work is founded upon personal empowerment to one's path of the heart, helping people align with new paradigms of belief, healing and expansion. She bridges diverse similarities and life's interconnectedness via her visionary approach. Amita is a seeker, writer, speaker, artist, gardener, admirer of the sacred and extraordinary honey bee, and avid nature lover spending much of her time within the beauty of Mother Earth. Amita lives in the mountains of Colorado.

Sam loved to longboard, snowboard, work out at the gym, go to the ocean and be with his close friends. He gave to others with is whole heart and brought a smile to everyone he met. He loved animals and spent his childhood and later years fascinated by all of nature, fearless in his interaction with snakes, spiders, insects, ocean life and all he encountered. He was a very talented artist creating through multi dimensional logo design and charcoal sketch. He is deeply cherished, missed and loved to the universe, the galaxies and back again as we told each other every day. Until we are together again...

10/13/1994 to 7/10/2014 Samuel Nigel Bacon

My Horse, The Hummingbird and A Very Small Tiger

The Pilgrimage

(Please Be Advised : Contains Sensitive & Sentimental Content)

Amita McBride

Since the initial writing of this book, there has been much change. Some of the adventure has been exciting and expansive and some of it has been constrictive and anguishing.

Galloping Grace Horse Ranch closed its riding program, which in turn brought my beautiful and dearest friend, Grandfather Joe, back home to me. Home to Colorado, that is, as I had changed my home base during his time at the ranch.

He did not come home alone. He had met his beautiful companion Robin, a mare whom had been donated to Galloping Grace for their youth riding program. Joe and Robin were deeply joined, heart to heart, one might say, and so I adopted her so they could remain together.

My anticipation was beyond description, to have my beloved Joe home with me and to meet Robin, the gentle, sweet girl I had heard so much about. As the trailer pulled up the drive and the ramp slowly lowered, tears of joy flowed freely down my cheeks.

Moving forward in time regarding all that has transpired since the initial writing of this book, a synopsis is essential. If I had known in advance all that would be experienced and how deeply it all connects to this book and my life path, well... it is possible this book would not have come into existence. Clearly, it was meant to be written, I have no doubt, for reasons I am not yet even aware.

I had my Joe and Robin for a time and then they both passed, transitioned to their next journey. It was a very, very difficult time for me. One of my cats also left during this same period.

Together with the loss of my dearest friend, Grandfather Joe, life took my most precious and beloved light as well: my son - my twin flame, my only child and the artist of this beautiful story. There is no language that could justly translate the emotions of my heart or the intensity of my journey.

The last several years has held me much of the time in deep silence and contemplation. I flew to France in the late Fall of 2015 and began walking over the Pyrenees mountains after barely sleeping or eating for weeks, my broken heart taking center stage. Wearing a pack I had not worn before, I began. All I knew was that I had to walk there, in that place, no matter what, as absurd as it was considering my state of being. She called me to her, to this Pilgrimage. I continued walking for many, many weeks. I walked and breathed, breathed and walked, sobbed and walked, walked and sobbed, repeating mantras with every breath, guided by and from my heart meditations. Powerful experiences and profound blessings somehow kept me going against all odds, against all forms of weather, through layers of exhaustion and pain, through sadness and anguish and finally through utter surrender.

I walked over 550 miles into the Winter, walking through part of France and into and through much of Northern Spain as well, walking the Camino de Santiago. I pushed myself on every level of my being, going further into myself, further into each moment, further into each step and breath that breathed me onward. Step after step after step on the ancient trail, I walked, preciously held by this sacred Camino. I was guarded and cradled within the millions of prayers of so many pilgrims who had come before, over 1000 years of hearts and souls held and guided by her grace.

The young woman who wrote the forward for this book, Emma Watton, walked with me but with great space between us. I had to walk alone, to be in silence, to listen. It was the only way I could agree to her companionship. I had traveled to Europe, pulled there, and was not expecting to have company. Though at times quite difficult, we were there for one another, a gifting for us both. Life has a most unusual way of surprising us, as I have shared in this book through many accounts. Not all that life brings forth is pleasant or easy, rather a testing of our strength, trust, self love and ability to honor what our inner calling is guiding us to do. All of this bringing potential for expansion and deeper unfolding.

It would be another book entirely to share the powerful journey these hundreds of miles unfolded. Sometimes in life, we are brought together with others for a brief encounter, others for longer, and a treasured few stay with us for a lifetime.

Emma's and my paths have diverged and no longer intersect. All in perfect alignment with life's unveiling.

It is time for me to begin the next leg of my journey, reconnecting with others through the path of the heart, helping, sharing, healing, *uniting. The Phoenix rises from the ashes to fly higher and lighter, shielded by grace.*

We are all shaped and molded by all that we encounter, experience and journey through - all that encompasses us, heart and soul. All of life is a pilgrimage, a Camino that we walk step by step and breath by breath. How we apply ourselves, how authentic we are with our feelings and state of being is the map guiding the outcome of our moments in time.

May each of you have the courage to listen to the voice of your heart. There is great beauty even in the depths of the hardest walk. We each truly serve a purpose, every one of us a cog in the wheel of the whole. How blessed I am to have been gifted such precious beings in my life. I honor them by continuing my journey, gaining strength by diving intensely into the love we shared and shall always share.

May Blessings shine upon each of you and all of life everywhere. May we show one another kindness and tenderness. We never know when the roles will be reversed and we will be the next one in need of compassion and love.

Amita McBride

February 2016

Grandfather Joe & Robin Winter 2014 Colorado

www.ingramcontent.com/pod-product-compliance
Lightning Source LLC
LaVergne TN
LVHW061159180325
806141LV00028B/928